Perspectives
Animals in Captivity
The Good and the Bad

Flying Start
to Literacy®

Contents

Introduction   4

My zoo home   6

Captive animals   8

What I like about zoos   14

Helping pandas   16

Boredom busters   20

What is your opinion?
How to write a persuasive argument   24

Introduction

Should animals be kept in captivity?

Have you ever seen a lion, shark or elephant up close? If it weren't for zoos, aquariums or wildlife parks, most of us would never get to see these majestic creatures. But is this a good enough reason to keep animals in captivity?

Many would say no! They believe animals should live only in their natural habitats.

But supporters of zoos argue that zoos and places like them shine a light on endangered animals, encourage conservation and carry out important breeding programs and other research.

How do you think animals in captivity should be treated?

5

My zoo home

Zoos help ensure that rare animals like this golden tamarin survive. They also keep animals in captivity because people like to watch them.

But are zoos like prisons? How can animals live well in an unnatural environment?

Why do we think we have the right to lock up animals for our entertainment?

Captive animals

Lucy the chimpanzee and Katina the killer whale are two animals that were kept in captivity. Lucy was raised by human parents as a scientific experiment, and Katina was kept at a theme park.

Their stories raise ethical questions, writes Kathryn Hulick. Was Lucy helped or harmed by growing up in a human home? Is there any way for theme parks to make life more comfortable for killer whales like Katina?

Read these stories and decide for yourself.

Lucy the chimpanzee

Lucy grew up in a regular house with adoptive parents . . . but Lucy was not human. She was a chimpanzee! Her adoptive parents, Maurice and Jane Temerlin, wanted to see how human Lucy would become, so they raised her as though she were a human baby.

The chimpanzee began her life with her adoptive parents as the subject of research, but she soon became like a daughter. She learnt sign language and seemed to truly care for her adoptive parents. Maurice, who was a psychotherapist, wrote in his book, *Lucy: Growing Up Human*:

"If Jane is distressed, Lucy notices it immediately and attempts to comfort her by putting an arm about her, grooming her or kissing her."

9

As Lucy grew older, though, life became difficult for the Temerlin family. An adult chimpanzee is about five times stronger than an adult human, and Lucy got into everything.

Eventually, the human "parents" decided to send Lucy to live with other chimps in the wild, at a nature reserve in Western Africa. Janis Carter, a student who had been helping take care of Lucy, went along to help the chimp adjust.

But Lucy didn't know how to live in the wild and her health suffered during the adjustment. Janis lived in the wild with Lucy for ten years. She ate ants and leaves to show Lucy what to do. Eventually, Lucy did start finding her own food, and Janis moved a short distance away. But then, Lucy went missing. When Janis and members of the reserve staff found Lucy, she was no longer alive and no one knows how she died.

The 20-year-old chimp had spent half her life in a human home and half in the wild.

Katina the killer whale

Katina is a female killer whale, or orca, that lived in the ocean off the coast of Iceland until she was two years old. Now, she lives at a theme park, where she regularly performs for huge crowds of excited onlookers. Katina is easy to work with, knows many tricks and has had seven calves.

John Jett, currently a marine mammal scientist who teaches at a university, used to work at the theme park and was one of Katina's trainers. He believes it's wrong to keep animals like Katina in captivity.

"It doesn't work out for the animals, and it's never going to work out for the animals," he says. "I think you can put all the money into bigger pools that you want but never re-create the ocean."

John explains that killer whales in captivity tend to experience social problems and health problems. For example, captive whales often chew on the concrete edges of their pools or the steel bars that separate different areas. As a result, most of their teeth are broken, missing, ground down or drilled out.

The whales may also float near the top of the pool for long periods. As a result, they may end up with a sunburn or a flopped-over dorsal fin – a common problem for captive male killer whales. The fins of wild whales are almost always straight.

Of course, life in the wild isn't perfect, either. In fact, a whale in the wild has about the same chance of surviving each year as a whale in captivity.

"Survival of killer whales in captivity has increased over the past 30 years," says Doug DeMaster, science and research director of the Alaska Fisheries Science Center. In addition, research with captive whales has added to our knowledge about their physiology and life history. On several occasions, scientists have used this knowledge to aid wild killer whales in trouble.

John Jett concedes that many theme parks have done some good for killer whales. "We no longer fear them," he says. "People have come to appreciate the need to protect them." He feels that the time has come, however, to stop keeping Katina and other whales captive.

Next time you're at a zoo or aquarium, think about what life must be like for the animals in either of those settings.

What I like about zoos

Read what these students think about zoos. Who do you agree with?

I love places like zoos and aquariums because they allow me to connect with animals I would only otherwise see on TV or in photographs. I am a strong supporter of these institutions because I believe that they bring to light the importance of conservation and the plight of endangered species. I strongly believe that if zoos and aquariums did not exist, people would feel less connected to the animals and would not care as much about the dangers that threaten wildlife.

Zoos are cruel places. Last summer, when I went to the zoo, I saw a white Arctic bear. Its tummy was green with fungus, and the bear looked hot and uncomfortable. Everyone was oblivious to the bear's suffering. Zoos are proof of human cruelty and ought to be extinct.

Zoos that care for animals properly are good places to see animals. There should be specific rules that a zoo has to follow, and if it doesn't follow these rules, then the zoo should be shut down and the animals sent to a good zoo.

I think that zoos enslave animals. They are enslaved because they aren't roaming free. Animals should be allowed to roam free in the wild. They deserve to be in their own environment unless they're hurt and need care. Even after that, they should go back to where they are supposed to live. Don't lock them up.

15

Helping pandas

The number of pandas living in the wild has dropped and they are in danger of disappearing forever, warns Rachel Young.

How can we support pandas and help save them from becoming extinct?

Protecting pandas' home

Giant pandas once roamed throughout the bamboo forests of China. There was enough land for wandering, and plenty of bamboo leaves, stems and shoots for them to eat.

But as forests were cut down to make way for houses and roads, pandas had fewer places to live. Without big bamboo forests, pandas couldn't find enough food.

Wild spaces called nature reserves were set up so pandas could roam in peace. But the number of pandas was still too low for the species to be safe.

More baby pandas

It was important to make sure that more panda babies were born and grew up healthy. That was a big job.

Baby pandas are born helpless – they're blind, pink and hairless – and they weigh about as much as an orange, so small you can hold one in your hand. For three months, a panda mother holds her baby almost all the time, nursing the infant to help it grow strong enough to find food on its own.

Panda mothers often give birth to twins. But in the wild, it can be too hard for a panda mum to feed and hold both babies. The smaller twin may die.

A newborn giant panda

Baby giant pandas

Zoos to the rescue

At zoos and research centres, however, people can help a mother panda care for both twins. As the mother nurses one twin, helpers called panda keepers take care of the other, cuddling the panda baby and feeding it from a bottle. It's best, though, if the mother can spend some time with each of her babies. So every few hours, the keepers switch the babies. That way, both twins get a chance to be fed and held by their mum.

Now that scientists in China know how to help care for baby pandas, the number of pandas in the world is growing. So today, the scientists have a new goal. They want to help pandas leave humans' care to return to the wild.

Returning pandas to the bamboo forests

But scientists can't just let the pandas go free in a forest. Pandas raised by keepers are not wild. They depend on their keepers, who make sure the pandas are healthy and have enough to eat. Wild pandas need to find their own bamboo to eat and safe places to sleep.

Baby pandas that are being trained to live in the wild can't get too used to their human keepers; otherwise, they may learn to seek help from humans instead of living on their own.

So keepers caring for these pandas wear special black-and-white panda suits whenever the pandas can see them. They make sure that their panda suits smell like pandas!

So far, only a few pandas have left their human helpers to live on their own. But one day, if more forests are restored and protected, there will be more safe places for pandas – and more giant pandas roaming and munching bamboo in dense forests.

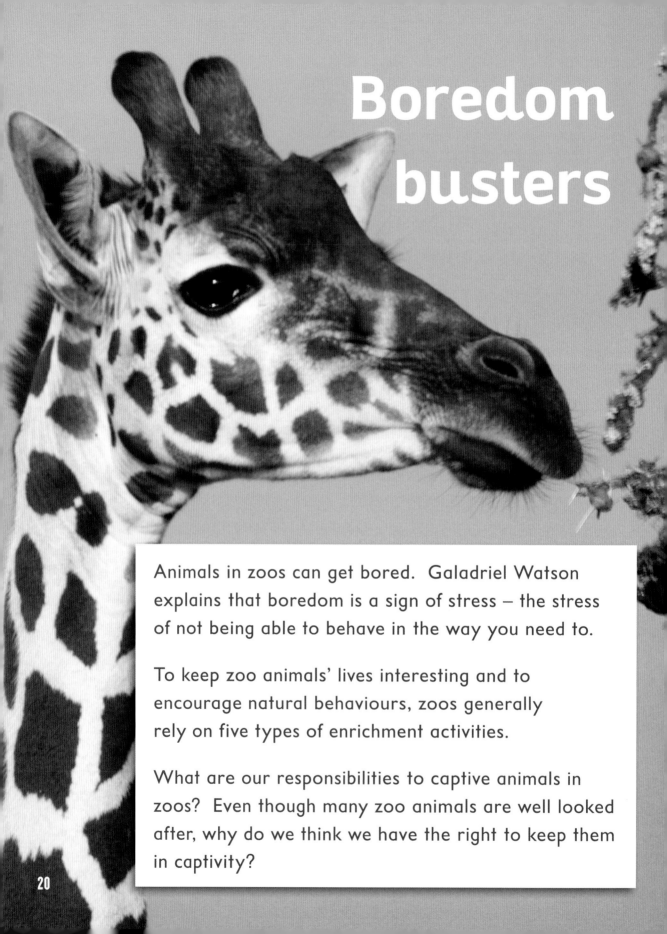

Boredom busters

Animals in zoos can get bored. Galadriel Watson explains that boredom is a sign of stress – the stress of not being able to behave in the way you need to.

To keep zoo animals' lives interesting and to encourage natural behaviours, zoos generally rely on five types of enrichment activities.

What are our responsibilities to captive animals in zoos? Even though many zoo animals are well looked after, why do we think we have the right to keep them in captivity?

1. Hang out with others

Some wild animals live alone, but many live in groups. If the animals are social, make sure they're grouped appropriately in the zoo, too. Place them with other members of their own species – and place them with other animals they would live peacefully with in the wild. Also give them plenty of zookeeper time so the animals and humans can bond.

2. Have a great place to live

Animals' enclosures must meet their natural needs, whether they like climbing, hiding, perching, swimming or burrowing. Give them animal-appropriate amenities like climbing structures, swings, caves and nets. Also consider the flooring – does an animal prefer mud or wood chips? And make sure the temperature and humidity reflect their natural habitats.

3. Engage all the senses

Sight, smell, hearing, taste and touch: make sure the animals are stimulated in all these ways. Scatter spices around the enclosure for them to sniff. Play nature recordings for them to listen to. Blow bubbles for them to chase. Give them scratching posts to rub against.

4. Work for dinner

Scatter food around the enclosure and make the animals hunt for it. Put the food in a tricky feeder and let the animals figure out how to get it. Throw the food on a mesh roof so the animals have to work to pull it through. The idea is to make feeding times longer and more difficult – like they'd be in the wild.

5. Think and play

Encourage the animals to explore and have fun with their mouths, claws, horns and other body parts. Engage their brains, too. Give them rubber toys, boxes, bags, barrels, tyres. Add excitement to an animal's day by hanging things up or tucking things away for them to check out.

What is your opinion? How to write a persuasive argument

1. State your opinion

Think about the issues related to your topic. What is your opinion?

2. Research

Research the information you need to support your opinion.

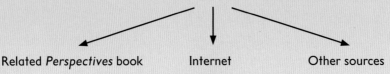

Related *Perspectives* book   Internet   Other sources

3. Make a plan

Introduction

How will you "hook" the reader?

State your opinion.

List reasons to support your opinion.

What persuasive devices will you use?

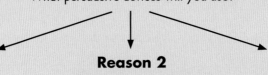

Reason 1

Support your reason
with evidence and details.

Reason 2

Support your reason
with evidence and details.

Reason 3

Support your reason
with evidence and details.

Conclusion

Restate your opinion. Leave your reader with a strong message.

4. Publish

Publish your persuasive argument.

Use visuals to reinforce your opinion.